STEP OF FAITH

INSPIRATIONAL POEMS

WRITTEN BY

DELORIS LOWE

McClain Printing Company
Parsons, West Virginia 26287
www.mcclainprinting.com
2004

International Standard Book Number 0-87012-715-2
Library of Congress Control Number 2004092709
Printed in the United States of America

Camera-ready copy supplied.

ABOUT THE AUTHOR

Deloris Lowe was born to Ted and Nita Hanna on November 6th 1957 on Fenwick Mountain in Nicholas County, West Virginia. She now lives in Fairview, West Virginia. She says she is just a country girl, living life to The fullest with God at her Side.

Deloris says she never wrote a single word until God came Into her life and it has never been the same since. She says That the words just seem to flow out of nowhere now.

Deloris enjoys writing poetry in her spare time or when God tells her to write something down. She hopes her Poems will help someone who feels there is no hope, she Knows from experience that life can deal you some nasty Cards, but she also knows there is help out there if you Want it. God is her light and salvation in good times And in bad.

Deloris hopes you will enjoy her book and will let the love Of God flow through you and take a step of faith if you Haven't already.

She dedicates this book first to God and then to her family And friends who are all inspiring.

LETTER FROM THE AUTHOR

Friends,

From the first page to the last, I share a little piece of my life with you. For in every word you can find me. I feel there is something in this book for everyone from the young to the old.

Most of all I hope this book will help you to find your way in life if you should happen to lose your way which sometimes can be easy and can happen without us even knowing it.

I have lost my way several times, but by the grace of God, he has been there to lead me, when I didn't know which road to take. He will be there for you too, if you take that step of faith, a step into the unknown where He has only been.

Thank you for sharing a part of my life and I hope we pass this way again. May God bless and keep you in His loving care.

Sincerely,
Your friend in Christ
Deloris

Deloris

MY DAUGHTER

I didn't know I could love,
Someone as much as I love you.
The day you were born I knew this was going to be a love
That lasted for a lifetime, a mother's love for her first Born.

I'm so proud of the little girl you were
And for the beautiful woman you've become.
You are truly a gift From God, one I'll cherish forever.

I wish I was more like you, you're so strong and you speak
Out for things you believe in. And you let people Know
You will not be stomped on. All these things I Wish
I was.

Don't ever change who you are and always be proud
And hold your head high, because you are someone and I
Love you.

If you ever need me, I'll always be here for the little girl
You were and the beautiful woman you've become.

To Nita, love Mom

MY SON THE SOLIDER

When he was a little boy he used to play with army men in
The bathtub for hours. Now he is in the United States army
With real army men, himself included.

He still has that little boy look, but he is all grown up. I
Still call him my baby boy and to me he'll always be my
Little soldier.

You ask, why am I writing this, well he is getting ready to
Go to a far away place, where God only knows what his
Future holds. As his mother I pray God will place angles
Around him and bring him back home to me safe.

He told me once I needed to let him grow, this I have done
Proudly and would do again, but as his mother I will never
Let him go. He will always be my little boy. I love you
Son!!

Shawn,

I love you more than life itself, and I'm so proud of you
that I can't find the words to tell you how much. Just know
with each beat of your heart, my heart beats also and we
will always be bonded to each other as mother and son.

Love, mom

OH, MARY

Oh, Mary what a mother you must have been.
She gave life to His Son, who would die for our sins.
Mary knew from the beginning how it all would end.
She smiled and in a soft voice said" I'd do it all again."

Oh, Mary you bore the grief
Oh, Mary you bore the pain
You watched Him die on that old rugged cross.
And life as you knew it was never the same.

Oh, Mary His Son came to earth to live as a man
Why is this so hard for us to understand?
You watched Him grow and you watched Him go,
To sit at His Fathers side, to think we can go there too if
In Him we'll abide.

Oh, Mary I'd want to be like you
You had faith in things, as He asks you to do.
You praised Him with each breath that you drew. Oh, Mary
I hope I'm half the mother you was
To walk by faith and tell of His love.

A FAMILY REUNION

There will be a family reunion over there, for we'll leave
Behind us all our burdens and cares. We'll look upon our
Loved one's face and walk in the glory of His grace.

The table will be spread out wide and the Lord at the door
Will be standing, calling us all to come inside.

We will bow our heads as our Heavenly Father gives
Thanks, for the food we'll be eating comes from chilly
Jordan's bank.

The angels will be singing songs of long ago, we'll all sing
Along for the words we now know.

Don't you want to join us up there be part of God's family
And in His love share?

A GIFT FROM GOD

Hannah grace was a gift from God for two people whom
Loved Him so. By praying to Him up above, He sent her to
Them out of His great love.

I know she'll love the Lord also for she will have many
Who love her and show her the right way to go.

Mom and Dad will walk beside her, and shelter her from
Life's heartaches, because they love her they'll do
Whatever it takes.

When the time comes for Hannah to spread her wings and
Fly, they'll tell her she can soar with the eagles on high, for
Nothing is impossible if you only believe and then give it a
Try.

To Jeff, Kathy, and Hannah Grace

A PERFECT LOVE

A perfect love is a love that will last forever, from the
Beginning of life to the very end. Not even in death can this
Love die. It has lasted until the end of time; to them it
Seemed like only a sigh.

I know this love was all to true, no it was not I and it was
Not you. This man and this woman a bond they did form,
No words had to be spoken, no hearts had to be torn.

These two walked side-by-side not one in front or one
Behind. The love they shared was for all time.

This man went first to walk the streets of Gold; the woman
Stayed behind, her children's hands to hold. She said it
Seemed like yesterday, she saw his smile so bright and how
She missed him, when she said her prayers at night.

For twenty years while he was gone, not any time did she
Stray, but their love was perfect, till their dying days. I
Pray they are together that their love goes on and on. This
Man And this woman were my Dad and Mom.

A RIVER OF HEALING WATER

There is this river I've read about and you can read about it
Too. It was written in the Bible long ago, just for me and
You.

It's said that there beside it on the east and on the west, the
Trees do not loose their leaves and the fruit it bears is the
Best

The river flows from north to south, and runs into the sea, I
Sit here and I wonder could this really be?

The fish they are many and the fisherman are more. You
Can watch cast their nets all along the shore.

Some day I'd like to go there and stand upon it's bank,
Giving praises for the healing water and giving God my
Thanks.

ABOVE THE GROUND

I was like a bird
I flew above the clouds.
I have seen a glimpse of Heaven
And I'm ready to see the Lord now.

Up above the water
High above the trees
I felt the spirit of the Lord
And cried, "Thanks for saving me."

If only all the world could see
The beauty made by thine own hands
They would surely realize
It was not made by a mere man.

My first airplane ride
May 04, 2003

ANGELS SINGING

I heard the angels singing the night before I died; they sang
When The Roll Is Called Up Yonder and In The Sweet By
And By.

I'm so glad I knew the Lord and let me tell you why. I'm
Going to be an angel and sing with Him on high.

I trusted in the Lord while walking here below and that is
My promise He made to me all those years ago.

He knew the time He'd come for me like all the He knows.
So, you better follow after Him wherever you choose to go.

In loving memory of Aunt Geraldine,
Who heard the angels singing.

BATTERED AND BRUISED

I've been battered and I've been bruised, I wonder how I
Ever loved you.
I was your wife, was it my fault you wanted to take my
Life?

You hurt me real bad, my life just seemed so sad. Thank-
God I had my children, they gave me a reason to live.

My eyes were black and my breasts felt bruised; I had
Never felt so used. You said to get over it; this is the life
You Chose. Oh, How little did I know?

No woman should ever feel used get out and start over,
Begin your life a new. Just say no to abuse.

Your special and God loves you.

COLUMBIA'S SEVEN

They were seven, which made them complete
They were called for duty, they knew where to meet
It was all for one, and one for all
They stood strong and they stood tall.

Columbia is up and away
The astronauts give one last wave.
They have seen the moon and stars,
And will live forever in our hearts.
They made the choice to soar in space
To do all they could for the human race.

They served us proud, one and all
Their love of God will forever stand tall
Each came from different walks of life
But they were one, when it came to that flight.
One by one they said their goodbyes
Not knowing it would be there last
Thinking only of the time they spend up there
Telling loved ones that they cared.

We can truly rest assured; they did not die in vain
Because they'll be others, to carry on their names
In memory of the crew
Of the Columbia space shuttle.
Gone, but not forgotten!

February 1st 2003

DEPRESSION

D-is for living in a deep dark dungeon where there is no light of Day or even being in the bowels of a fire-breathing dragon.

E- is for finding that there is no way of escaping this terrible way of living or even wanting too.

P- is for trying to find that place where you can have a little Peace without trying to please everyone except yourself.

R- is for people reassuring you not to let it get to you and not knowing what it they are talking about, or caring to know.

E- is for others saying that they got through it and it was easy Which was a lie, no way on earth could it be.

S-is shame on me for letting it get this far, without reaching out for help.

S- is for simply choosing to go through it alone.

I- is for insane, which I sometimes think this world is.

O- is for only having to pass this way once, because I couldn't go through it again.

N -is for needing a friend, I can't do this alone. Help me Please!

Depression is a terrible thing to go through, I know because I think at one time or another we all find dark spots in our life when we become depressed. Don't let anyone fool you in to Believing It's easy, because it's not, and don't be afraid to ask For help, that's why it is out there to use in Time of need. Don't let it take away the you, the one you used to be. He or she is a Good person, just find them again.

DID I THANK YOU TODAY?

You gave it to me
Your love so unconditionally
You showed me to care
And that you'd always be there

Did I thank you today
For each breath that I take
Did I thank you today
For the love you have gave

Did I thank you today
For the things you took away
Like the pain and the fears
The hurt and the tears
And replaced it with a smile on my face.

Did I thank you today
For helping me find my way
For now I can see
What's been waiting for me?

Did I thank you today
For each smile on each face
Did I thank you today
For taking my sins away.

To say thank you seems small
Like it doesn't matter at all
But you know that it does
Because I say it with love.

DOVE CRY

Have you ever heard the mournful cry?
Of a dove,
Calling for her lost love
Did he just fly away?
Will he come back another day?

The pain you can hear in her song
It tells of something very wrong.
Did he meet a new dove?
Did he forget about his first love?

She gave him her everything
Her heart and soul
And took him under her wing.
She even taught him how to sing.

She say's she'll never be the same
But I know she'll be good as new
Because the Lord is going to see her through.

ECHO OF TEARS

You could hear them crying long after they were gone.
Their tears still echo in the early hours of the morning,
Telling us they never heard the warnings.

As you walk by, the place where they lost their life,
Whether it's day or whether it's the dark of night.
You'll get a chill, even though the wind you never feel.

These brave men never stood a chance that dreadful day on
That ship.
They never dreamed it would be their last trip.

The ones that did survive, they tell their story.
Only they say the ones you hear crying,
They deserve all the glory.

Dedicated to the soldiers who died on the battleship
"Arizona" on December 7, 1941 at Pearl Harbor.

ENDANGERED SPECIES

You've heard how the dinosaurs
Have become extinct.
Well it won't be long before that's us,
So what do you think?
As Christians we'll no longer exist,
Do you think when were all gone?
That we'll even be missed?

I want to be able to give thanks
To the Lord and to pray,
But they are people out there
That wants to take that right away.

You're afraid to say, "God bless you
And I'll keep you in my prayers."
Afraid because people don't seem to care,
That as Christians
Our love of God we are trying to share.

When the time comes that they tell me
I can't profess my love for my Savior and Lord.
Then I don't want to live anymore.

That's when we'll go
On the endangered species list
Never to live any more.
We don't want that to happen
So stand up and fight for the Lord.

EVERYDAY IS CHRISTMAS

Everyday is Christmas when Christ lives in your heart.
It goes on in the afternoon and even into the night.
That's what Christ is all about.
He's 24/7,365 days a year.
Can't His voice you hear?

It's in the birds that sing, the bees that buzz,
And in the wind that blows through the trees.
He is even in you and me
All we have to do is believe.

It's said that's a hard thing to do.
How do you know He exists?
You believe in other things, so believe in this.
For Christ is Christmas!
Without Him there would be no holiday.
No star to light the way!

FIGHTING FOR JESUS

Who will you stand for when the time comes?
Will you stand by the Father and walk with Son?
We can win this battle,
When all the storms rage.
We'll hit them hard,
With the rock of ages.

From up on the mountain tops,
Or in the valley low,
Whether it be raining,
Or whether it be snow,
We'll live to fight another day.
And walk along life's narrow way.
But, we must walk hand in hand.
If we're to protect the Promised Land.

God has built a fortress,
In all our hearts with love.
Remember He sent His Son to us
From somewhere up above.
He will come back once again,
That's why I'll fight for Him
Until the bitter end.

FIRE

One flicker or one flame
And all you own
Will go down the drain
And life as you know it,
Will never be the same.

Where does it get its start?
Is it Mother Nature?
Or is it man made?
All it takes is just one spark.

The heat it can be unbearable
As if you're in Hell,
Where did it start?
No one wants to tell.

So, don't put your life savings
In earthly things below
Store them up in Jesus
And to Hell you won't have
To go.

FREEDOM AND PEACE

The eagle stands for freedom
The dove it stands for peace
You sent them both from above
So we all could know of Your love.

You shed your blood on Calvary
It washed my sins so far away.
You made me white as snow
And Your love inside me began to flow.
Like the waters that won't run dry,
My love for You will never die.

You never have to walk alone
If you serve the Lord,
Then Heaven will be your home.
Just give up the things of this world
For they will all pass away
But the Lord will always stay.

We all can live in freedom
And we all can enjoy His peace.
Because God's love is forever
And that will never cease.

FREEDOM

Freedom is blowing in the wind
You may see her flying high or
Even flying low, but she will still
Be flying no matter where you go.

She is everything we believe in
Even when times are tough,
Just like9-11 she will never ever give up.

She has stood the test of time
In war and in peace.
But her enduring freedom
It will never ever cease.

She will go on standing
Until the end of time
Not only does she live in your heart
She still lives in mine.

FROM DUSK' TIL DAWN

The frost was laid out like a blanket on the ground,
As the steam was rising up all around.
The smoke from the chimneys filled up the sky,
Even the fall leaves were swirling
Silently from up high.

Shadows were darting in and out that cool morn,
Just waiting to see
If the sun was going to come out and warm.
There was only a slight breeze,
Even then there was no need.

The homes I passed by
They had no lights,
The people were sleeping, still thinking it was night.
Not a dog barking or even a cat in sight.

The night creatures, were running to get out of sight,
Telling each other to have a good night.
Right then the rooster began to crow, saying to everyone it
Was time to get the show on the road.

GETTING OLD

I've heard from my elder that getting old sucks.
That their bodies are sagging
And they have to be nipped and tucked.

Their hair color comes from a bottle
And some say they would just like to have hair
Others say they just don't care.

They say they are doing their best.
What's that you say
You have hair on your chest.

I hear I can't see a thing
On the top of your head,
No I said it's time for bed
How about I'm loosing my sight,
And I can't hear a thing.

Oh, Well I'm alive or at least I think I am
I carry my eyes in my pocket and my teeth they stay in a
Can, my ears are in a cup
When you get to be my age you hope they fix soup to sup.

Getting old is not for a sissy.

GETTING OVER

I got over you a long time ago
You're no longer a part of my life
I remember when you said you loved me
And asked me to be your wife.

You ask, is it yes or is it no
Will you stay or will you go?
I was young and I said yes
I told you I'd give my best.

Our life together soon began
I'll never forget the day you took my hand.
I thought I knew who you were
And what you were about.
Little did I know our home would never be a house?

A house is a place of love and warm fuzzy feelings
Not a place where you are all alone,
Even when there are people around
And you feel like you're about to drown.

So, I got over you and I've moved on
And I love me and who I am
There are no more tears, and I know now that I can.
For I have no more bad, all I have is good
You say you love me, well I guess you would.

GOD'S PEACE

I sit here waiting for peace to come,
I keep quiet, but I hear none.
The leaves of fall, rain all around me,
But still no peace comes.

Is my pain so great, that I am missing the blessing?
I should receive? Should I wait longer for God?
To send the peace I seek?
Do I fall apart and die inside
Or fight for peace, which decides?

Like the colors, all around me;
I see myself in each one.
But still no peace comes.
The colors they are many;
Burgundy, like wine, gold like the sun that shines,
Brown and plain; like my pain. There is some green,
But for me I know not what it means.

Is my pain and grief so strong, that I cannot find
Where I went wrong?
Am I right or are they? Where is the peace I need?
Where is the me I used to be?
Help me find her if you can!
I know you will, you're the Son of God.
I sit here and wait for peace to come.
I am quiet, what's this I hear
A still small voice speaking to my heart,
"You've had the peace you seek from the start
It was buried in your pain and grief.
The peace you need is always near
Just listen again to your heart."

GOD'S DECORATIONS

You can see God's decorations everywhere
They're all apart of nature.
The colors they are many
From reds and blues and greens
You can see them every season

In the spring the grass is growing
Up out of the ground, how not knowing.
The trees are all budding,
The bulbs are peaking out of their beds.
In the summer
When the flowers are blooming
What a wonderful sight to behold
The smell it is so awesome,

In the fall the world is lit up
When the autumn leaves are changing
The gold's and browns, Burgundies and bronze
Keep falling to the ground.
In winters the ground if frozen
From all the fallen snow,
The snowbirds can be seen all around
In the trees of green are the red cardinals
And the screaming blue jays
Even the crows are getting in on this scene.

There is no need to buy pretty lights
Or lots of colorful ribbon
Just take the time to enjoy the decorations
That God has given.

GOING HOME

Mom and Dad have already went home,
And our two big brothers too.
We are left here below
Waiting till it's our turn to go.

I'm not talking about our earthly home
I mean the one above.
The one the Bible talks about,
That is filled with so much love.

I'm told it is a mansion
With streets that are pure gold
Are Mom and Dad happy?
Do they think of us here below?

I know if I keep the faith light burning
And live by our Heavenly Father laws
I will go to see them
When the Lord makes another house call.

GRAND GLORIOUS MEETING

There is going to be a grand glorious meeting
Waiting on us over there.
Where in God's grace were all going to share.
All my loved ones who have gone on before
Will be happy when we walk through Heaven's door.

The music will be playing low,
As the angels are singing songs, we all know.
We won't know the day from the night,
For we'll all be basking in His glorious light?

If you want an invitation,
Just receive the Lord as your salvation.
This meeting is in the air,
And brother I sure hope to see you there.

HE KNOWS MY HEART

The singers were singing,
Songs we all love to hear
I could tell the Lord was visiting
By the comfort that was near.

As I went to the altar
To bow on my knees and pray
It started shaking, why I could not say.
The tears flowed all out of control,
And the Lord spoke to me
And said "your story's been told."

I said, "How could this be,
Nothing was said at the altar that day."
He said, "I know what has never been spoken
I also know your heart has been broken."

His voice said, "I've known all things
Since before you were born,
I've been with you all along.
I was just waiting for you
To call on my name,
You did and now your life
Will never be the same."

HE ROSE UP

He came down, down, down
But He rose up
There isn't a job here on earth
That's too tough

Yes, He came down, down, down
But he rose up
If you walk alone
The road will be rough.

Hand in hand, step by step
You'll walk this road
Trusting in the Lord,
He'll lighten your load.

He came down just for you and me
That is why He hears our every plead
I know He did not die in vain
So I'll call upon His name.

We rose up out of the miry clay
I can still remember that day
He was nailed to that old tree
How in this world can you not see?

HE'S COMING AGAIN

The Lord is coming back once again
Will you be ready to meet Him then?
Have you listened to His holy word?
And in Him have you chosen to serve?

No this path will not be smooth
It will depend on the way you choose
The road is rough here below
But it will be worth it
When with Him you go.

Just remember what He's done for us
Now that had to be really tough.
Who of us would give our son?
For all this world's sin
Just like our Heavenly Father did.
I would guess to say, He'd do it all again.

HIS LAST MEAL

The table was spread out wide
As He called His disciples to come inside
He said, "There would come a time
When the crowd will cry crucify, crucify.
And I'll lie down my life and die."

It was to be His last meal
For He knew he was going to be killed
He sat at the table with his friends
Telling them how His life would come to an end.

"I was sent here to tell you of my Father's great love
From the beginning I knew I was sent from above.
Don't cry when my life has ended
For yours has just begun.
Because you listened to my Father,
You will now walk with His son.

Go tell others about His mercy
And about His great love.
For they will be no others like me
Who will come again?
It's up to you to tell the world
How it all will end."

HIS TRACTOR

He went down the road on
His John Deere tractor,
And in his voice you could hear the laughter.
He was taken back to when he was
A little boy, who had just received,
A new Christmas toy.

In his eyes were tears of joy,
For he was no longer that little boy.
God had made his dream come true
He said he did this for me
And he can do this for you.

Now that I am a man,
I use my John Deere to work my land.
I plow the fields and I sow the seeds
I try and do all good deeds.
For I will reap just what I sow
And on my tractor I will go.

When I die my John Deere tractor and I
Will go work gods garden in the sky.
Since I did well while here below,
There won't be weeds up there to hoe.

Dedicated to my husband,
Jerry Lowe

HOW DO YOU GET TO HEAVEN

How do you get to heaven?
Well you can't take a car
A train or bus.
You can only get there by the Father
And only through His trust.

The trip will not be easy,
For the road it can be rough.
The mountain can be steep
And the valley can be wide.
But if you trust in the Lord,
He'll take you to the other side.

You can't buy a round trip ticket
For there is only one way to go,
The map was drawn up long ago
And the way was written in stone.
The directions are in the Bible
In case you didn't know.

I'm going to take that trip to Heaven
When it is my time to go,
And look upon His face.
For I trusted in His word
And I was saved by His forgiving grace.

HOW LONG

Just how long has it been?
Since I've seen you last
And how long has it been
Since the sand ran through the hourglass?
I can't believe it's been four years
Since we said goodbye
It has been too many years
Since God gave you wings to fly
It only seems like yesterday
That I saw your smile so bright
And how you kissed me on the head
When going to bed at night.
These are the things that I hold so dear
To me now that you are gone.
They even keep me warm in life
When it comes a raging storm.
I never really understood just what you meant to me
And now that you are gone
It's very plain to see.
I think about you every day
And look at pictures too.
Oh, But what I wouldn't give
To have a moment to spend with you.
To tell you face to face just how much I love you.
If you could know what's in my heart,
I truly apologize
For not being the person I thought you wanted me
To be.
I now know, no matter what
Or how my life will be
I am everything you saw in me
When it was I who could not see.

I CAN'T REMEMBER

Time has stolen my mind away
There are times I can't remember the day.
It sometimes makes me sad,
Cause I can't remember the good times I've had.

I think I have kids you see
Their pictures sit here and look at me
Some days I have two,
Other days I have four,
I don't know I may even have more.

Have I always lived alone?
Is this really even my home?
I have questions, can't you see.
Cause I can't even remember me.

Oh, What I wouldn't give,
To be young again.
Then I'd think about how my life would end.
My children get upset at times,
They know deep in their hearts,
I have lost my mind.

This is dedicated to the families of those
Who have a loved one who is suffering from
Alzheimer's.

I LOVE YOU

I wrote I love you in the sand
And when I got the picture back
Standing in the shadows was an
Image of a man.

I tried to think who could it be
That had been watching me.
For there had been no one there
And all I could do was look at
This picture and stare.

And in a while it became quite clear
It had been God standing so near.
It meant more than words can say
That He was with me on that day.

It's a comfort just to know
That God is with me wherever I go.
He'll go with you if you ask Him too.
For He loves me
And He loves you.

I'M A NEW ANGEL

I'm a new angel, I just got my wings
He gave me a voice and now I can sing
He told me to trust Him and I 'd have everything
I'm a new angel, I just got my wings.

I'm a new angel; I'm learning to fly
I know how to laugh and I know how to cry
I've already lived, but my soul will never die
I'm a new angel; I'm learning to fly.

The world is my heaven, my home is up above
And I know through believing, this place I'll be leaving
I was saved by His grace, and washed in His blood.

I'm a new angel, I just got my wings
There not very big, they can hardly be seen
I know they are with me, by the love that I feel
I'm a new angel; I'm learning to heal.

IM JUST A MOTHER

I'm not a singer or a writer; I'm just a mother
Some one to turn to when life gets you down
I'm a human being with feelings and with pain
I'm just a mother

I wonder why God gave me such a wonderful daughter
I sit here and try to understand why,
You cry and why things are the way they are
I don't know those answers; I'm just a mother

When you hurt my children, I hurt too
Because I'm just a mother.
There are many of us here, who are just a mother
And can feel my pain and share in it too
Because we're just mothers.

My son, is in a foreign land, and war may be upon us
He makes me proud, because I'm just his mother
God chose me, to do this job, to take a baby boy, and turn
Him into a great man, and I'm just a mother.
To some, that may not seem like much
To me, it is a lot, because you see, he's the only son I've
Got

And God, had a son too and Mary, was just a mother
A mother's love never dies! It just keeps getting stronger
And stronger, with each new generation. You ask me how I
Know this?
I'm just a mother, who had a mother who loved me

J-E-S-U-S

J-is for He died **just** for you and me
On a cross long ago on Calvary.

E-is for life **eternally**
He'll give if you only just believe.

S-is for our **sins** set free
And we'll be free indeed.

U-is for **united** we'll all be
And live like a true family.

S-is for our **Savior**, we'll see
And bask in His glory we'll be.

Put them all together they spell **Jesus,**
A word that means the most to me.

KATY

Her ears are so long they drag the ground.
There's not a better darn dog around.
She sure acts like a lady
And yes her name is Katy.

She lies on her belly
When she eats her dinner,
And she could be
Just a little thinner.

Her legs are short
And she is as wide as she is long
When she howls
It's like she is singing a song.

She wouldn't bite a flea
For she is slow as she can be.
She doesn't know a stranger
But boy she will run from danger.

She is my best friend
And I'll love her till the end.
When she dies I pray she'll go
To doggie heaven in the sky.

In honor of Katy, my best friend

LETTERS HOME

They said, "Dear Momma,
I love and miss you so.
How I wished I was back home
Sitting on the front porch swing,
Listening to you sing that song"

He also mentioned Poppa
Said to say hello and how he'd like to fish in their favorite
Fishing hole.

How is sister he did ask?
Tell her she better not give you any sass.
Tell her I love her too,
And to keep on playing the blues.

I'll be home again real soon,
It may be morning, night or noon.
Then we can do the things we love,
And give the glory to God above.

It's hard to be so far from home
And in another land. I look
Out my barracks and try to understand.

How can we be who we are when the lights of home, they
Seem so far?
I know one day these things I'll know
Because God tells me so.

Well Momma, I have to close and turn off the lights.
But all of you will be in my prayers each and every night.

LIFE'S SCARS

My body bears the scars of a sinner.
My eyes you can see all the pain.
Until a loved one told me about Jesus,
Now my life has never been the same.

No I don't hide the scars that life has dealt me.
As I am the one who chose the way I would take.
See, I listened to others just like me,
So these are all my mistakes.

I'm glad I heard about a Savior,
Who would make me white as the snow
For no matter how dirty, He loved this and me I now know.

LIGHT

There is a light at the end of the tunnel
At times it may be hard to see
But if you put your trust in the Father
It will be there for you and me.

Life can be dark as a dungeon
Or as bright as the morning sun
It all depends on how strong your faith is
If it's the dark or the light you will see.

You may be high on a mountaintop
Or down by the rolling sea
But no matter where you are in life
He will walk with thee.

The wind will blow and the rain will fall
Just remember who created it all.
Even in the roughest wave or hardest storm
There is a light to see
It's like the coat of many colors
You ask what could it be?
It's a rainbow shining bright
For all of us to see.

So no matter if it's day or night
Remember God can and will be our
Shining light.

LOVE AND PAIN

Did you know that love and pain are two of the same? They are joined, where there is one you will always find the Other. I know this to be true, since I feel that from people Who say they love me and hurt me at the same time. So, Do they really love me or do they like to cause me pain? I Can't answer this question can you?

Sometimes I can't tell the two apart. I don't know where Love begins and the pain ends. This is such a hard way to Live, not knowing if they care or are they just pretending? Would you like to live like this? It gets pretty hard at Times. For me, when I say I love you it is for keeps. Why can't it be this way for others?

Yes, I am searching for answers to these questions filled With pain. I can't seem to find where the love comes into Play. Please if you can hear my pleas help me find the Answers I so desperately need. They say you know all, if This is true; I am calling on you to stop the pain and bring Me love again.

These words are meant for you, you know who you are and You know the pain I feel. They say they love me and Would do what it takes to make me happy; if this is true Love one another as you both say you love me stop causing This pain. Give me back my love, that's all I need.

MILK AND HONEY

We live in the land of milk and honey
We should be happy,
But all people think about
Is how to make money.
They're always trying to make more,
While the rich get rich
And the poor stay poor.

What ever happened to people sharing?
And to the people who were
So loving and caring?
Have they all died?
Is no one willing to try?

Now I'm not rich and I'm not poor
I'm sure we all could use a little more.
I've got more than I've ever had,
I've had a mom and I've had a dad.
I don't need much when I go to the store
I have a Heavenly Father who could
Ask for any thing more.

I've got a loud spirit
And I'm not afraid for people to hear it.
I'd ask a stranger to enter my door,
For I'm not rich and I'm not poor.
I'm not afraid to give to others
As he has given to me,
I wished that were how we all would be.

MOM OR DAD

God gives to us a child to make our own
Remember, that we reap what we sow
Plant the seed of love and kindness
Always keeping Satan far behind us.

They will be just what we teach them
So teach them goodness instead of sin
Teach them to show respect and
Teach them never to neglect
If you will do your part
God will teach them from His heart.

Always love unconditionally
No strings attached and God
Might send us another batch.
To love in good times or in bad,
God chose us to be a Mom or Dad

MOMMAS' GARDEN

Momma has gone to be with Jesus
Do they have a garden there?
Will momma grow her roses?
Will the Lord keep them in His care?

While momma traveled here below
Her garden always seemed to grow
No matter what the weather would be
Her flowers grew continuously.

Her children were like her flowers
Each needed a different touch
All needed lots of her love
Others didn't ask for too much.

Momma worked hard in her garden
She never let it get her down
If something didn't grow
Cause she gave it all her love
For this one thing I know.

In loving memory of Lorene Lowe

MORE THAN A FRIEND, A BROTHER

He was just a young man,
All those years ago.
Now his hair is as white as snow
He is not just a friend of mine,
He is like a brother
I hope he knows I love him
And there could never be another.

He has gone the extra mile
He's been there through my tears
And even through my smiles.
When I was a little girl
He made me feel real big and
Now I am a big girl he treats me like I'm small
To say the least, he has been there through it all.

I've known him most all my life
We've shared heartache and pain
And if I had it to do over again
I'd do it just the same.
No matter what I had to say
He took the time to hear.
And he's been there through all my years.

TINY
I'll miss you when your life on earth is spent
Cause you're an angel sent from heaven
To be my friend and my brother.

MY DAD

My Dad held his family together
Just like super glue.
And when times got tough,
He got tougher too.
Mom was the house, all nice and warm
Dad was the foundation,
That held the house together
When came a raging storm.

Dad worked hard
To put clothes on our backs
There was plenty of love
That we did not lack.

What I wouldn't give
To hear the sound of your voice
Saying good night
Or telling us kids, it's time to turn off the lights.

There is no doubt in my mind
That God needed you up there
Probably for children
Who didn't know a dad
Had so much love to share.

In loving memory of Ted Hanna

MY FUNERAL

I want to have my funeral before I die
I wonder will people laugh
Or will they cry.
I want to see the look upon their face
When I set up and state my case.
Will they look in my casket?
Or will they walk on by?

I don't want lots of flowers
For they will fade away
Unless they're artificial,
Then they will stay and stay
And stay.

I hope the preacher isn't long winded
For people will lose faith
They will sit and they'll wonder
How much more of this can I take.

Just put me in the ground
And throw the dirt right in
For I'll have left long ago
Just to be with Him.

I want my funeral to be happy
Not sad.

MY BROTHERS AND SISTERS

My brothers and sisters
Will stand beside me through thick and thin,
And my brothers and sisters will walk with me,
Until my life comes to an end.

My brothers and sisters share my highs and lows
My brothers and sisters I love them a lot,
And Lord I hope they know.

In the years that have gone by
They've gone their way
And I've gone mine.
But, I think about them all of the time.

I wonder do they think of me,
As much as I do them.
I surely hope they know
I'm so glad God made us kin.

I dedicate this to my brothers and sisters,
Lester, Charlotte, Libby, Mildred, Mike, Bill,
Dave, Connie, Jackie.
With all my love

NEVER ALONE

Whether you're standing on a mountain high
Or walking in the valley low.
Remember you'll never travel alone,
I'll be with you wherever you go.

Whether the sun be shining bright
Or in the cold dead of night.
You will know that I am there
Because of this bond we share.

As the snow falls silently to the ground
All you have to do is look around.
And I'll be there by your side
Cause my love for you will never die.

When the storms are raging around you
Please do not fear,
For my voice you shall hear
I am walking with you
I am always near.
You are never alone
Because I am your light of home.

NEW BIRTH

They said congratulations,
I heard there was a new birth.
Was it a boy or girl?
And was this your first?

I smiled and said thank you,
But you don't seem to understand
See I had to die, so I could be born again.

I was given years ago
To my mom and dad
And by the look upon on their face
I could tell that they were glad.

Then I grew up and went astray,
For the Lord I did not know.
I'm so glad I got the chance
To be born again.
Now I can till the seeds I've sew.

NO HOME

She had no home to call her own
No shoes or socks
The only home she had
Was an old cardboard box?

She asked herself how could this be?
I live in America, the land of the free.
But for me it is not free any more
I'm down on my luck.
I can't even buy food from a store.

My food comes from out of a can
The kind you find trash in.
I don't think I have one friend.

Then I got turned on to the Lord
And thing are looking up
Not down anymore.

I have a warm place to sleep
And food on a real table to eat.
Yes, I still feel sometimes like I'm lost
But I know God paid the ultimate cost.
So I don't moan and complain,
I just give thanks in His name.

NOT FREE

We say we live in freedom
But it is not free.
It comes with a high price
No matter what you believe.

Some will lose their life
When they pledge to serve,
Knowing this could be the sacrifice.

They are our sons and daughters
Going off to war, fighting battles
Not fully understanding what they're
Fighting for.

I'm glad to have my freedom,
And the ones who proudly give
To make this all possible.
Are you glad for what they did?

The next time you see a soldier
Smile, and give them a salute,
Say just a little something for all
They do.

NOT IN HEAVEN

No prisons in heaven
For your sins have been forgiven
No ball and chains
You've been saved by His name

No need for hospitals
They'll be no sickness or pain
Your life in glory land
Will never be the same.

There will be no transportation
For you will not want to leave
Because in Heaven
God will supply your every need.

The weather will be sunny
We'll have picnics everyday
And the Lord will share this with us
And we'll bow our heads to pray.

Can't you just imagine how this all will be
Everyone will love everybody
As we walk beside the crystal sea.
We'll all walk hand in hand
On the streets of gold
And share the old ,old story
That was written long ago.

NOW I CAN SEE

God took the blinders off
And now I can see
All I needed was to have faith and believe
I thought the world was right
And nothing was wrong
Until the Lord talked to my heart with a song
Now I see the beauty that surrounds me
That I never knew was there
Lord how much have I missed
When I didn't seem to care?
I pray every chance I get
For more blessings from above
That God will always touch me
With His undying love.
I know I have to be willing to give
Him all that I am or will ever be
Because He is the one who
Took the blinders off so I could see
He is the one who paid the price
For you and me
When He died on that cross on Calvary
The price I have to pay
It seems so very small
Because it is He who gave it all
My life may be full of mountains high
Or even valleys low
But I will never walk alone on life's
Rough and rocky road.
I could never find my way
In this world below
If it wasn't for my Lord

ON THE OTHER SIDE OF THE MOUNTAIN

On the other side of the mountain
Not so very far from home.
That's where I met my Savior
One night while all alone.

He said if I would trust him
My sins would be set free.
And my soul would live forever
In His home eternally.

My life has been so different.
The changes have been good.
So when He comes to call me
I'll go where Calvary stood.

The cross it's still standing,
The wood faded and worn.
I can feel the love around me.
Just like when I was borned

And if you'll walk beside Him
The way I'm going to do
You'll live in that mansion
That He's built for me and you.

ON THE WINGS OF FREEDOM

On the wings of freedom,
I'm going to fly.
I can choose to live,
Or I can choose to die.
I have that choice that others did not,
They lost their life, but not in vain.
We're a country of love,
We'll live to fight again.

This is a battle we did not choose,
We can win this one or we can loose.
We'll stand strong till the end,
We will not break and we will not bend.

One by one we come together,
For better or worse we'll fight however.
We can be weak or we can be strong,
But this thing called terrorism,
It's just plain wrong.

The time was set, the date was too.
We knew it was coming,
Just didn't know when.
This was done at the hands of other men.

So, on the wings of freedom,
We're going to soar.
The sounds are loud,
You can hear them roar.
Whether it's day or whether it's night,
They started this war
And we're going to fight.

OPEN THE GLORY GATES WIDE

Open the glory gates wide
Bring your hearts come inside
Open the glory gates wide
Jesus will be by your side

I have just started to fight
For the man that gave me my life
I walked through the gate
What a beautiful sight
Jesus was waiting inside

The battle has begun
I know it can be won
The man they gave me life
He'll help me win the fight

I saw Jesus holding a light
As He said to me, "it's alright."
He held out his hand
And He said, "Good man
My son you've won the fight."

OPERATION FREEDOM

Somewhere out there another land exists
It doesn't live in freedom
It's a land ruled by the fist.

They fight for God and country
So all may live in peace
And in our hearts, we want the war to cease.
Our flag for freedom flys,
And that will never die.

If we are to be victorious
And live to fight another day.
It's time we as a free nation
Get on our knees and pray.

Nothing is made possible
Unless God is on your side
Our soldiers serve our nation
With their love and pride.

We will not falter and we will not fail
We go with God and we will prevail.

REMEMBER MY CHAINS

Brother Paul said, "Remember my chains
For I wear them in my Father's name."
He walked through trials and tribulations,
For the love of all creation.

He was beaten and bruised
For the old and the new.
He did this for the many
And he did this for the few.

How many of us would do the same?
How many of us
Would wear those chains?
To live and to die in His holy name.
For me I'll remember Paul's chains
I too am responsible, and I am also to blame.

Oh, How we like to forget
Their pain and their suffering
But the Lord says, "Not yet."

SOMETHING TO SAY

She was ninety-two when she made her way to speak
You could tell she was frightened
By the tears flowing down her cheeks.
Her voice was just a whisper
It could barely be heard,
She knew we would hold to her every word.

"I have something to say,
I'll try and hurry and not keep you here all day."
She said, "When I was a little girl,
My hair was black and not one curl.
Now it's white and I am old
But listen to me; I have a story that needs told.

The man that stands accused
Could not have done such a thing
For see himself as a child too was abused
All he ever wanted to do was sing.
But he was always being used.

So believe me when I speak,
And please set him free.
For he is my son, and is not guilty of any crime
It is I who should be punished; it is I who should do the
Time."

SPIRITUAL ROCK

A spiritual rock everyone should have one
It can be the Father, or it can be His son.
I know who mine is, because my life is His.

I gave my life to Him three years ago
And He has been my rock
Even when times are tough and the road it gets rough.

What do you think of when I say rock?
Maybe large, maybe small
Some say I cant see it at all.
Others say hard and it will break.
I know God won't give you more than you can take.

He can be your rock
And your shelter from a raging storm.
He will be a shoulder to cry on
He will be in good times and in bad.
I'm so glad He's all I have.
The Lord is my rock and my salvation
He not only represents the United States,
But lives for all nations

STANDING AT AN ALTAR

I was standing at an altar
When I heard a sweet voice
It said, "Come to me child
It's time to make a choice".

Can you see Him standing there?
In His robe of white so fair.
Can you see His smiling face
And do you know His amazing grace?

Is He knocking at your door
Will you ask Him to enter in
Or will you let Him pass you by
And let your soul continue to die.

Jesus said, "I am standing
At an altar of prayer
And He said, "My child I'll
Be waiting for you there.
With my arms open wide
Inviting you to come inside.'
I'm so glad He was waiting for me there.
Standing at an altar of prayer.

STORIES

Here are a few stories I'd like to share,
They tell of God's love and how much He cares.

You heard how Daniel was thrown into the lion's den.
Did you know they didn't eat him?
The Lord closed up their mouth
And Daniel walked out of their house.

Did you hear about Jonah?
Whom did a fish swallow?
How about when God led Moses out to teach.

What about Noah, who built a big old ark
And about the animals,
Who came two by two
Before the door was shut at dark?
How it rained for forty days and forty nights
With no land in sight?

My favorite is when He'll
Come again, to gather all His sheep,
To take them to live with Him in glory
If in His path we keep.

TAKING TIME TO PRAY

When I'm in a hurry and I don't take the time to pray.
Everything I am doing just seems to go astray.

But, when I take just a moment to give thanks to the Lord.
My day just keeps getting better than all the days before.

Yes, they'll even be more worries
Than you will ever know,
No one said it would be easy while walking here below

The load it can even get lighter
Not even to hard to bear.
Because you trusted in the Lord
He'll help because he cares.

So take just a moment each and every day,
To say thank-you for your saving grace,
Turn that frown into a smile for it will help you go that
Extra mile.

TALKING TO JESUS

Precious Father plead for me
For you know what is in my heart
You've known it from the very start
Speak the words I cannot speak
Heal my heart that does not beat.

I know what I want to say
It's been with me forever and a day.
Why are they so hard to speak?
Is it because they're too hard to hear?
I fear that I might break or shed a tear?

Help me Lord! Please lead the way
I may get lost, I may even stray.
These words I know you long to hear,
I can't say them because of my fear.
It's hidden deep inside my soul,
I'm afraid of warm, for all I know is cold.

Hold my hand, why I cannot say.
Show me Father and teach me to pray;
So I may walk in the light of day
Forgive me Father I've lost the way.
I need to find that peace and love.
That can only come from you above.

THE BLACK SHEEP

In this flock there were ten sheep,
And two shepherds.
All the sheep
Felt they belonged to this flock,
Except one.
She was the black sheep of this family
Even though her coat was white as snow.

The two shepherds tended the sheep
At different times of the night and day.
They fended off whatever dangers
Might come their way.
Hoping that none of their sheep
Would go astray.

All the other sheep made fun of the black sheep
Making her feel bad,
So this little black sheep was always sad.
The black sheep always did her best
And gave all she had to her mom and dad.

The black sheep left the flock,
As others went their own way too.
Now the black sheep
Has put her trust in the Lord
And does as she is told.
For she is going to be with others like her
And live among God's fold.

THE BOOK

There is this book wrote long ago
And in another land.
The Lord spoke the words,
But it was written down by just a man.

This book tells of good times and of bad,
How some gave little,
And how others gave all they had.

It tells about the beginning
And speaks about the end.
It tells us all about this old world's sin.

It tells how things will come to pass
And of things that He made to last.
Every house should have this book,
And when times get tough just take a look.

It tells how we can be set free
And live with God eternally.
You can hand it down from generation
To generation,
You can share His love
From nation to nation.

If this book you cannot find,
Let me know I'll lend you mine.

This book is the HOLY BIBLE

THE CHOSEN ONE

Our heavenly Father knew long ago,
He'd have to give His son,
To die on an old, rugged cross for everyone.

His son was born to Mary,
She loved Him as her own.
She knew one day she'd have to give Him up,
For this was not to be His home.

He came and lived and died for us
So we could live in His trust.
He was known as the chosen one.
Would we do the same?
I fear not one, in His name.

He even knew how this world would be
And he still let His son die on Calvary
He surely must know something that we don't
For I would have given up on us a long time ago.

THE COAL MINERS PRAYER

Each day before I go to work
I bow my head and pray
That God will give me a safe trip to work
And keep me safe all day.

I sit in this place as the darkness overcomes
I feel I am not alone,
I can feel a presence with me
I ask how can that be
The others left long ago
Their lights I no longer see.

My prayer is God will keep me safe
And again I'll see the lights of home
I know through faith, trust and believing
I will not die here alone.

One day the water came pouring in
And I thought my life at an end drew
But by the grace of God
He saw me safely through

One by one we all came out
To loving arms above
The world was all with us
Cradling us with their love.
Remember when I said before
I know I'm not alone
God was here beside me
And He brought me safely home.

THE COMMUNION

This is my body broken for you
This is my blood; I shed for you too,
And I would gladly do it all again
Just to save you from your sins.

I gave my life on Calvary
So you could have life eternally.
The way will be long and the way will be rough
Believe in me and it won't get too tough.

No mountain is too high and no valley too low
Because you have trusted in me
I'll walk with you wherever you go.

When your life is over
And you've went the last mile of the way
The angels will greet you
And we'll all fly away.

THE DAY OF THE LORD

The day of the Lord is coming,
I can hear it in the wind.
He's coming
To take those who trust Him,
Away from this world of sin.

Will it be tomorrow?
Or will it be today?
Who of us knows for sure?
Who of us can really say?

It's best if we are ready,
To meet Him in the sky,
Then we can all go together
To that sweet by and by.

THE DEACON AND HIS WIFE

The deacon and his wife are quite a funny pair
And when you are around them
You can't help but show you care.
Neither ever wears a frown,
They always seem to smile.
And if someone is in need of help
They go the extra mile.

God has truly blessed them
In all they do for Him.
A long and happy life together,
It will never end.
They lift each other up to God each day,
And they always take the time to pray.

Their life has been a light,
To others along the way.
What a crown of glory
They'll share when it comes to their last day.
They don't brag and they don't boast, they say
It is the Lord that deserves the most.

I'm so glad I know these two
They have blessed me in a way my life
Will never be the same.
And all of this they gladly do
In our Father's name.

DEDICATED TO JOHN AND MIDGE GREENE

THE DREAM

I woke up this morning with a song in my heart
And a smile on my face.
I had been dreaming of a different time,
And a different place.

The time was in the future
The place had streets of gold
And I knew I was in Heaven
From all the stories I'd been told.

The fields had different flowers
And the blooms they smelt so sweet
And all of God's creatures were sitting at His feet.

There was glory all around Him
And Jesus sat on his right side.
He was telling about His love
And how we all should abide,
How we all could live forever
And never have to die.

Then in a flash, I was awake
I said, "oh! No it has to be a mistake.
I want to close my eyes and dream again
Of this place that has no sin."

THE FISHING PIER

Have you ever been on a fishing pier?
When the tide was rolling in?
What stories you can hear,
The tales they never end.

You've heard about the big one
That got away,
Or how about the one
You caught just yesterday.

Let me get the camera,
Don't let this moment slip by
I'll take a picture with your fish
So you can't tell a lie.

And when they ask you
Where are your fish today?
Just simply tell them
It just got away.

THE FOUR WINDS

There are four winds that blow,
And this one thing you should know.
One comes from the east, just where the sun is rising,
One comes from the west where the moon it is dying.

The other two come from the north and south.
These winds are blowing from our Fathers house.

These winds can make the trees sway,
Or make the waves out on the sea roll.
They can even make the bells toll.

These winds they let me know the Lord is near,
And he hears my every prayer.
I'm so glad He took the time to blow my way
And to show us that He cares.

THE GLORY OF GOD

The glory of God can be seen all around
It can be seen in the trees or even on the ground.

From the tiny hummingbird
Who looks for something sweet,
Or from a silly bull frog,
Who seems to jump ten feet

How about the tree so high
With all its branches stretched out wide.
Or how about the moon and stars
That fills our night skies.

What about a sunset
Like you've never seen before,
Or that pot of gold
At the end of a rainbow
When down the rain pours.

Even the rushing wind
That makes the trees sway
Or when you ask Him
To come into your heart to stay.

His glory can be found
When you're not looking for it.
It's there for the entire world to see
Aren't you glad He gave it to you and me?

THE HEALING

The walls are not falling
The roof does not leak
The windows aren't shattered
It's the people that are weak

The pews, they set empty
The people have all gone home
The piano sits silently
It's not playing a song.

The altar in front stands idly by
Not one person kneeling
No one is willing to try
To talk to the father
Who lives up above?
Do they really know Him?
Do they know of His love?

Only by praying and fasting too
Will this body of Christ, be good as new
The Bible says ask and it shall be given
Go to the Lord, because He has risen.

THE HEART OF A RAINBOW

People ask, where does a rainbow end?
I want to know where a rainbow begins.
It's colors can be seen everywhere.
I think God made the rainbow for all to share.

Others ask what about that pot of gold
I say it's in the beauty, which the rainbow holds.

Does a rainbow have a heart?
Is that how a rainbow starts?
Do the colors beat from end to end?
Like our blood flows from within.

I saw a rainbow in the heart of a tree
Could God have put it there for me to see?

The colors were so bright,
They could have lit up the night.
The red was crimson, just like wine
The green was the color of grapes,
Right off their vine.
The blue was bluer than the sky.
The yellow was golden like the streets up high.

The next time I see a rainbow
Of this I will remember.
For in my heart I know that God was the sender.

THE HEART OF A VOLUNTEER

There is nothing as strong as the heart of a volunteer.
Who's always ready when trouble is near?
They will be ready when tragedy strikes,
Doing whatever it takes to make wrongs, right.

They came together on 9-1-1,
Doing what it took to get things done
They were there to save someone.

Some will carry them through
Others ask what can they do.
They will give their all
Just to answer the call.

It does not matter if their life could end
They just want to help a friend.
Their shoulders are very wide,
But their hearts are twice that size.

These people do not know a stranger
They're not afraid of any danger.
We all can be a volunteer
All we have to do is be there when someone
Sheds a tear.
And ask, "How can I help you
And you're not alone.
I'll do my best to get you home."

In honor of all who volunteer their time.

THE HOLY KISS

The holy kiss is a kiss between Christian brothers
Or maybe a kiss between sisters and mothers
A holy kiss is a kiss like no other.

It can be a kiss from a friend
Who says they'll stick by you until the end.
Maybe it's a kiss between a mom and a dad,
Thanking each other for all that they have.

Or possibly a kiss from sister to brother
Who is going off to war,
They're afraid that they
Will see each other no more.

I think a holy kiss is like no other
Saying more than words can ever uncover
A kiss from our Heavenly Father to His Son,
Telling him what a wonderful job he has done.

So, greet someone with a holy kiss today
And see if it won't
Make them change their way.

THE HOLY MOUNTAIN

I'm going up to the Holy Mountain
Where my soul will never die
I'm going to drink from the love filled fountain
That never will run dry.

I fell as low as I could go
But now I'm looking up,
Up at the holy mountain
And the Lord's is going to fill my cup.

I have stumbled in my life
Thru sickness, sin and shame
But He reached down from the Holy Mountain
And touched me in His name.

Leave your cares behind you
And come and go along
We'll go up to the Holy Mountain
Giving praise to the Lord in song.

I'm going to put my trust in the Lord
And do as I am told
For I've heard about the Holy Mountain
And the beauty that it holds.

THE HOUSE

There was a house built long ago
And in another land.
God made the blueprint,
Man did all the work by hand.

The house was long,
The house was wide
There were many rooms inside.

There were many doors
And many gates,
The floors were golden,
And silver was the plates.

For in this place a king would dwell
And reign for evermore.
For see this place I talk about,
Is the house of the Lord.

THE HUMMINGBIRD AND THE BEE

The hummingbird and the bee
Flying in and out of trees
They fly high and they fly low
Knowing not where to go
The bee it can sting
Just like the hummingbird it has wings

These two creatures they are small
One's not short and one's not tall
They're around in the summer
Not the fall.
Sometimes you never see them at all
In the winter they fly south
I'd like to keep them at my house

The bee it can sting
And the hummingbird hums cause
It can't sing
This is a quite unlikely pair, cause
One has feathers and one has hair
And you know what is so funny
They both seem to like honey.

If I could only keep just one
First I want to know where they come from
I think they came from God above
Sent to us out of his love.
He created them for the world to see.
He even loves the birds and bees.
I love them both can't you see
Cause without the hummingbird
Where would the bee, be?

THE LIGHTHOUSE

The lighthouse is still standing,
The walls are battered and worn,
The light it's still shining,
When it comes a raging storm.

The beacon it's still working
To warn all the ships at sea.
They would loose their direction,
If it wasn't for my light they see.

I have never seen it,
But I'm told it is there.
No one mans the lighthouse,
No one seems to care.

If I were a ship's captain,
Or just a passerby.
When a storm came upon us,
Would we live or would we die?

The storm rages around me,
The sea tosses me about.
It would surely claim me,
If it wasn't for the lighthouse.

THE MESSENGER

One cold and winter night I was awakened by the thought that someone or something was watching me. I lay there for a moment and held my breath, almost afraid of what or who it could be. I slowly turned toward my bedroom window, and as I am looking out, there is another set of beautiful brown eyes looking back at me. It is a whitetail doe; she says she was sent to me to give me a message. The message is to tell me she has been where I've been and everything is going to be alright.
I lay there and I wonder how does this creature know what is in my heart, she says God knows all about it and has sent her here to help, to let me know that I am not alone. I am with you always. This is not to say you will not have valleys to go through or high mountains to climb, but I will help you and never let you fall behind.

First, you must trust in me and look for me in the night when you're feeling all alone. Just call out my name and I again will appear at your window, as all the nights before, see I've been here all along just waiting for you to need me and say, "Lord I need your help I can't do this alone anymore" I ask myself am I weak because I need help? He says the answer is no it just means you are one of my creations and are asking your Heavenly Father for guidance and my child that is all I've ever wanted from you is to need me.

So, now every night I look out my window and I feel safe. Because I know that the little whitetail deer is watching over me and is there to help me through whatever the problem may be. She is the messenger sent to me by God.

THE MOUNTAIN OF THE LORD

Come; let us go up to the mountain of the Lord.
There's no need to walk
In this valley anymore.
The way will be long
And the way will be tough.
We're not the only ones
Who've had it this rough.
What is has already been.
As long as there is life,
There will always be sin.

Go to the Lord, daily in prayer
And He'll take the walk with you
Because He does care.
The mountain may be low
Or the mountain may be high,
But if you listen to the wind,
You'll hear the Lords' cry

God wants us all
To come up to the mountain.
There the grass is green
And the waters are golden
That flows from the fountains.
Don't be afraid of what you can't see
Just remember, what is, always will be.

THE OCEAN AND THE SEA

Have you ever seen the ocean,
When the sun was going down?
It will take your breath away,
No better scene has been found.

Every time I look out across the sea
I wonder is there something, or someone
Looking back at me.

The sound of the rolling waves
As they pound against the sand,
Has stood the test of time,
Before there was even a man.

I always stand in amazement,
At what the Lord can do.
He made the sand and sea
And he made you and me.
There is no place I'd rather be
Than by the ocean or the sea.

THE PASSER-BY

He was just passing by
Going no place at all
He paused for just one moment
To hear
A group was giving God the praise

Then in that one moment
God spoke to his heart.
And said my son
Here in this humble place
Your service to me
Is about to start.
He said, " how could this be
For I do not know you
I'm just passing by"
The Lord spoke to him and said,
"For you I have died."

"Go back to your homeland
And tell others about me,
How I was born in a manger
And died on a tree,
So all their souls could be set free.
Tell them how you were just passing by
And how I as your Savior, spoke to you
From on high.

Tell them to just believe
That I am all they'll ever need.
Tell them on Me to rely
And their souls will never die.
And how you were just a passer-by."

LEAVING THE PAST BEHIND

How do you leave the past behind?
And get on with your life.
When others use your past
To cut just like a knife.

No, I'm not perfect
Who here can say they are?
Because of our past
We all have to bear our scars.

My life has not been an easy one
The pain and loss I've carried
Sure feels like a ton.
But by the grace of God
He'll help me through the past I've trod.

I try to take it day by day
Only one step at a time
Asking the Lord to help me when I pray.
And Satan tries to ruin the way
By putting the past back on my mind.

The Lord he forgives me
And loves me anyway
Why can't others do the same?
And put the past away.

THE POETS

Each came from different walks of life
Just wanting to perform their best.
They spoke different languages,
But yet they were the same.
All were giving praises in their own way
To His Holy name.

Some spoke of trials and tribulation
Others about their life situations.
The words spoken could be happy
Speaking volumes about their joy,
Or they could be sad,
Telling how their life turned out real bad.

For them it wasn't about winning,
It was wanting to be heard
They wanted the audience
To hang on they're every word.
They had a story that needed to be told.
It was like the birth of a new baby,
Everyone wanted to hold.

My first poetry convention

THE PREACHER

He is not big
And he is not small
But when he preaches
He stands ten feet tall.
He reaches out to one and all
I'm so glad he heard the call.

Preacher Dave is his name
Saving souls is his game.
He sure is blessed in the spirit
And if you don't believe it
Come to church on Sunday
And you can hear it.

He is more than a friend to me
He's my brother in Christ you see.
He'll be there through thick and thin
And he'll be there in the end.

God bless you preacher Dave!

THE RAGING SOUNDS OF WAR

As the lighting flashes across our sky
The bombs are bursting over there high
The roar of the thunder,
It shakes the ground.
The glory of God is heard all around.

The wind it makes the trees sway
But our troops, they fight another day
Our God will smite the enemy
With His hands
You can hear them run to foreign lands.

The rain it turns the sand to mud
Just remember in Noah's day
There was a flood.
We can live or we can die by the sword.
It all depends if we serve the Lord.

The hail and snow falls from above
It comes to us through His love.
This tells me God is on the throne
And I'd never make it on my own.

THE SCROLL

The scroll was rolled up tightly,
With words written of long ago.
It was closed with seven seals,
No one was to know.

The day will come,
When the seals will be broken.
And those words will finally be spoken.

No one knows when that time will be
We're told of things that will happen,
Things we don't want to see.

The Bible says they'll be riders,
On seven wild horses
Riding through the sky.
And how all the unbelievers
Are going to die.

So, now you better get ready
While you still have the time.
So choose God as your Savior,
Before He changes His mind.

THE SECOND SEAL

As the second seal was broken
He spoke in a voice of authority
Out of the clouds riding on a fiery red steed
Came a rider who would take away world peace.

This was a plague coming in the end of days.
Father would fight against sons
Brothers against brothers
And daughters against mothers
This war would be like no others.

When this rider, rode across the heavens
He waved a great sword
And said that there would be peace no more.
For the earth would soon pass away
And our Father in Heaven
Was coming back to stay.

This horse and rider did not roam alone,
There was one before him
And five after,
Who came and went
Each with a plague
Much worse than the first.

We say we want world peace,
Well we're not doing what it takes
To cause this evil to cease
We need to teach others God's way.
The seal has been broken;
Can things change for the better?
Well that's what I'm hoping.

THE SHEPHERDS

Have you heard about the shepherds?
Who lived so long ago?
And how they followed their flocks
Wherever they would go.

They tended their sheep in the day
And slept with them in the fields at night.
It did not matter where they went,
For the shepherds would go there too.
Those shepherds could be me or you.

If believe in the Lord
And do as we are told.
We can be good shepherds and lead
Lost sheep into the fold.

THE SOLDIER

They are our protectors
Our sons and our daughters
Our mothers and our fathers.
When was the last time I said thank you
For laying your life on the line
So I can live in freedom and enjoy mine?

Let's not take them for granted
For they receive no awards
When the wars are over
We'll forget what they have done
But they will not forget,
Who fought right beside them
They will forget no one.

In time some say they'll forget
And go on with their lives
But I think I should not forget
For it doesn't seem quite right.

Now I want to take the time
To say thanks for what they've done
They fought for God and country
Some will never hear those words,
For they never made it home.
But for those who will live on
Thank you, thank you
One more time.

THE SPIRIT

The spirit of the Lord speaks to my soul
Just like the blooms of the flowers
As they all unfold.
The sound of the wind is angel wings beating
Telling you to God's word you better be heeding.

Who knows how long he'll call you to come.
Don't be deceived, because there is just one.
There are many out there
Who spread the word?
But they alone will not be heard.

Only by God and born though His Son
Washed in the spirit
Will the true words of the Lord
Be spoken so all can hear it.

Don't wait too long,
For they're playing your song.
Don't sit idly by,
While others are moving
Stand up to the spirit
It's the Lord you'll be choosing.

THE STORM

There is a storm brewing
It comes from deep inside
Will it come up slowly, Or like the changing tide?
It flows from top to bottom
Never knowing when it will rain.
The only thing this storm knows is that it has to stop this pain.
The wind begins to dance
The sky from blue turns gray
Lighting runs across the earth the thunder rolls on high
Will the storm come raging in or will it pass on by.
The water it comes raining down
From the sky above.
Trying hard to hide this place by the raging flood.
We ask ourselves how will this end?
Will the rain keep coming down
Or will the sun shine again?
This storm depends on you and me
As to how it will die.
Do we fall apart or do we continue to try?
The rain is our tears, and our eyes are the sky
The lightening is our words the thunder is our cries
Help us Lord to calm this storm
We can't do this alone
Together with your love
We can make this house our home.

THE STORY TELLER

There is a story teller Here among us all today
He uses his stories to show us the way.
They may be from his childhood or even about today
They're sort of like his road map
To show his life's highway
Each story that he shares with us
Could be words of heartache or pain
They also show us through Christ's love
We will never be the same.
When he was a young man The Lord he did not know
But through the prayers of others He trusts Him here below
The road he said was rocky
Many obstacles along the way
He said he was so glad His mother took time to pray

The storyteller can make you laugh or even make you cry.
But you can tell he loves the Lord Even when he sighs

I'm so glad he took the time
To pass this way you see
Because I hope his stories touch your heart
The way he touches me.

Dedicated to John Jones,
I'm glad that he shares his stories with others.

THE SUN AND MOON

The sun was rising in the east
And the moon was shining in the west
I ask how could this be,
It had to be one of Gods best.

It was early in the morning
When this was taking place
I could tell others were surprised
By the look upon on their face.

Some said it was a harvest moon
Others said it was a tequila sunrise
All I know was that I
Could not believe my eyes.

Was this a sign they talk about?
That will come before times end,
Maybe God is telling us
That there should be no more sin.

I will never look at the sun and moon the same
For I wonder will we see this again.
The day they both decided to shine
Or will they be lost
For no one to find.

THE SWEETEST SONG

I woke up this morning singing
Since Jesus saved my soul
Now I'm rejoicing
For His love has made me whole.

The birds they too were singing
Just like the angel's do.
It was a song I've never heard
It had to be brand new.

It was the sweetest song
To my ears, its words they spoke
Of how God is so near,
And that if we believe in Him
We should never have any fear.

I got down on my knees
And thanked the Lord he had chosen me
To hear this song they sang so sweet
Then the birds they flew to sit
At my dear Savior's feet.

THE UNITY TOWERS

The twin towers majestically kissed the New York skyline,
along with the Statue of Liberty.
These were symbols of what America stood for.
Because of terrorism, the towers are not there anymore.

Our statue of liberty is still standing strong, telling
everyone who believes in freedom, that Bin Laden was
wrong.

Terrorism just didn't hurt America that day
Many other nations suffered the same way.
Even people from his homeland, this was so horrifying
No one to this day can understand.

Many lost their lives that day
From New York, Pennsylvania to Washington D.C.
We're still trying to figure how this could be.

The towers may be gone, and our loved ones will be missed
dearly, but when found bin laden will be punished severely.

You ask why unity towers?
Well because side by side they stood tall
And side-by-side they did fall.
Neither left one to stand-alone
Both went down together in unity
Both took our loved ones home.

THE UPLIFTED VEIL

The spirit was written in my heart
God knew this from the very start.
It was covered for years with a veil,
No one knew it was there, only God could tell.

It was nothing like a wedding veil
But like the one that Moses wore,
The kind that could touch the floor.
Because of God's glory read, 2nd Corinthians
It will tell you the story.

If we believe and trust in His name;
He will take our veil away.
But if we choose to ignore the signs,
We will be among the perishing when comes our time.

Remember through God is our only salvation
Not just for us,
But for all of God's nations.

THE VALLEY OF DECISIONS

I've been down to the valley of decision.
Trying to decide what road to take.
If I take the left one,
Where it ends I do not know.
If I take the right one,
The Lord I will have chosen.

Do I go and trust in Him,
Or should I go astray?
Do I continue to walk in sin?
Or live with Him in grace?

If I decide to walk away
And live in this world of shame,
Will He pass me by,
And never call my name?

THE VALLEY OF DRY BONES

Have you ever been so low
And had no place in which to go?
Well, I've been there myself
A time or two.

My body it felt broken
And my heart it would not beat
And my aching bones
They could not stand the heat.

Then I heard about this valley
Where the bones they were dried up.
And how the Lord spoke to these bones
And told them to get up.

And in a flash they began to rise,
And He blew His spirit in their face
They opened up their eyes
And looked upon the Lord,
Who raised them by his grace.

He'll do the same for you and me
If in His word we'll trust
We may be in the valley of dry bones
But he's going to lift us up.

THE VISION

The Lord came to me in a vision
One day while all alone.
His voice said, "I have a story to tell you,
That never has been told.

There is this place that all can go,
If in Me they'll believe.
The streets they are pure gold
And there are mansions by the sea.

Close your eyes and you will see
All the beauty there,
And you can lay down all your burdens
And your cares.

There the four winds blow,
And the sun it always shines,
Follow Jesus and this can be
All yours and mine."

I thought that I had, had a dream
And none of this was true.
Then I read the Bible,
And this one thing I knew,
God was here to guide me and help me
Safely through.

THE VOICE

Speak to me Heavenly Father
For I long to hear your voice
I'm so glad many years ago
I made you my choice.

You are in the sun and sea
I'm so glad you rescued me.
I see you in the moon and stars,
I know your love is not far.

You speak to me when I'm asleep
The words I hear they are so sweet,
You know the words I need to hear
They comfort me to know you are near.

I hear your voice upon the wind
And in the rain,
I'm so glad you share my pain.

Someday I'll see the face
That goes with that voice,
Oh, How my soul will rejoice!

THE WOODWORKER

When he was a little boy,
He liked to play with wooden toys.
He held them in his tiny hands
And wondered all about their plans.

Now this boy is a man
And the wood he now understands.
He can take a piece of wood,
Hold it in his hand
And see the beauty there
Just like God had planned.

What I wouldn't give
To do the things that he can do
With any piece of wood he holds.
You can see it in his eyes
A piece of wood he loves.

Dedicated: to my husband, Jerry
Who can take a piece of wood and
Turn it into a work of art.

THIS PLACE

What happened to the world we know?
Where did all the beauty go?
The birds, the deer, all God's creations.
This has to be another nation.

There is not one here I should know I
Looked for them where did they go?
Dear God I pray,
Bring back the beauty to this land.
Don't let it die from other hands.

I hear the wind, I see the storms
You calm the sea where waters rage
Let us live like we used too
Bring back the peace and love from you.

I sit here silently and wait to hear you speak
What's this I hear You say, "I have
The wind, the storms at sea
You say these are all words from Thee."

Now, I see a deer, a bird, and a tree
Thank you Lord for loving me
The beauty of this land has been restored
And so has my love and faith in you Lord.

THROUGH MY DAUGHTER'S EYES

Why can't I see me,
The way she sees?
She says, "Mom you're so beautiful."
I ask how can that be?
When I look in the mirror
That's not what I see.

My eyes well up with tears
For all I see are all my fears.
There's heartache and pain,
All in front of me like a large bloodstain.

She says, "Mom you're great."
And all I feel is hate,
Not for her, but for me.
She says, "She sees love in my eyes."
All I see are the lies.

She says, "I'm her hero."
All I am is a zero.
I've done nothing, and I've been nowhere
She says, "I don't care.
And that she loves me."
And I know that's all I need.

TIMOTHY TEDDY BEAR

Hi, my name is Timothy
And I'm your guardian angel bear
God sent me down to you
To show how much he cares.

If you want you can take me to bed at night
And hold me really, really tight.
I'm here for you when you feel bad
And even when you feel sad.

I'm an angel, and I can fly
But be assured I'll be at your side
So if it's day or if it's night
I'll love you with all my might.

I went away for a little while
But now I'm back in a different style
I'm still me and I'll always be
The one you loved unconditionally.
Remember God sent me to you
And I'm here to help you through.

In memory of Timothy Lowe
Who left us way too soon.

WALKING WITH UNICORNS

I've been to the land
Where unicorns roam free
Would you like to go there with me?
Their beauty is so rare,
There is only one thing
That even can compare.
And that is the glory of the Lord.

You say how can this be
There are no such things.
I say, yes they are;
I've seen them in my dreams.
They were so very many
They were eating by a rolling stream.

Some were solid white
Some were as dark as night
Some had horns of silver,
Some had horns of gold,
I tell you this was a sight to behold.

You can see a unicorn too
Just close your eyes and believe.
That is all that you will need.

WAR SOUNDS

As the snow falls silently to the ground
The sound of war is all around.
The question is will Saddam comply,
Or will he fill us with his lies?

We as a nation, have lives at stake,
How many of our loved ones,
Will this war take.
Other wars have claimed many
I don't think we should have to lose any.

These soldiers are our sons and daughters,
Sisters and brothers,
Mothers and fathers.
They made the choice to fight for our flag,
To defend our freedom and all that we believe in.
They'll stand tall and give their life
For us all.

There should never be a war
For peace should rein forever more.
Bring them home one by one
They served us well,
Their job is done.

WAVES

The waves come rapping at the shore
Just as Jesus comes knocking at your door
Who will come to get you?
When it comes your time to go
Will it be the angels?
From somewhere up above
Or will it be a serpent,
From somewhere down below?

The waves go up and the waves go down
Just like the highs and lows of life.
You can be on a mountain in the day
Or in a valley on a cold dark night
All in all it's very simple
You only have to choose
You're the one who has to decide
What you have to loose.

The waves come in
And the waves go out
The Lord you can depend on
And the devil, he gives you doubt.

But like the rolling sea,
The tide it can be gone
So make your choice,
And do it now
For tomorrow may not come
You're the one who decides
If the sun you shall see rise.

WHAT IF

What if God only loved me and didn't love you?
What if the sky was black instead of blue?
What in the world would we do?

What if the world was square instead of round?
And the moon stayed up and never went down?
What if the sun never did shine and we
Could not ever change our minds?

What if the grass was brown instead of green?
And you yourself could never be seen?
What if there were no mountains or no seas
Where in the world would we be?

These are the places that I go when I feel
Like no one cares, do I dare ask have you
Ever been there?

What if we all lived here?
And what if God
Or others did not care!

WHERE WILL YOU BE WHEN THE TRUMPET SOUNDS

Where will you be when the trumpet sounds
Will you be ready when the Lord comes down?
Will you have answered when He called?
Or did you pay no attention at all.

The trumpet sounds loudly
For Christians everywhere
Faces light up for they know that He's there
And they'll be ready to meet Him in the air
They know God's coming and He cares.

Oh, What emotions there's laughter and tears
Some are going home, others have to stay here
They didn't heed His voice and
They didn't make the choice
I'm so glad I heard the trumpet sound.

So, if you're not ready
Then you better prepare
You know that He loves you and you know that He cares
Now is the time stand
Come out and join our Savior's band.

WORDS AND RHYMES

He gives me words and He gives me rhymes
They're not yours and they're not mine
It is His way to let us know,
We're being thought of here below.

They can help you heal and cry and mourn,
They can help you smile and even grow;
These words come from God, don't you know.

Some are small ones, some are big
Some I don't understand,
Some I can't even speak.

You will know where they come from,
By the meaning that they hold.
He will help you to use them,
If you do as you are told.

They may come to you all at once,
Or even one by one.
But you will know they're from our Father
And from His only Son.

My prayer is that He'll speak to you,
The way He speaks to me.
Just have faith and trust and believe,
And He will give to you words and rhymes.
Remember though, they're not yours
And they're not mine.

YOUR CROSS

How heavy is your cross?
Does it weigh you down?
Does it make you feel lost?
If you trust in the Lord,
He'll carry it for you
No matter the cost.

Jesus died our cross to bear.
We're never alone,
He is everywhere.
Our Heavenly Father
Gave His only Son
Our battle on earth,
He has already won.

We can decide how heavy it will be.
By the choices we make,
Will it be short?
Or will it be tall?
It's your decision
It's your call.

Are your burdens hard to bear?
Give them to God, because he cares.
How heavy is the cross you carry?
Take it to God and do not tarry.